120 Super Fun Activities

for babies, toddlers, and kids up to six

Indoor, outdoor & travel games, making crafts, ...

Table of Contents

0-18 months

18-36 months

3-4 years

4-5 years

120 Super Fun Activities for the Little Ones

Children often have a lot of energy. The little ones in particular are always looking for new discoveries. But how can you, as a parent, easily manage this kid's energy? What games can you imagine for your child without buying up the toy shop? And how can you find the balance between playing with your offspring and organizing your daily life?

This book contains a whole series of games for infants to preschoolers. You'll find activities geared to your child's developmental level that will help you understand how your child grows and changes and how your playtime together can enhance learning. You'll be able to play with your child in a way he or she really enjoys from the very beginning!

Before explaining the games and activities, we would like to give you some tips:

- Every child develops at his own pace. In this book we give you the averages. That means that things can be different for your child.

- Kids don't need to have expensive toys to amuse themselves. Often they have fun with everyday materials like cardboard boxes, plastic bottles, and old clothes. Instead of getting rid of these things, save some for your treasure box of play materials!

- Playing with your kids doesn't mean putting the housekeeping on hold. This book contains a lot of ideas on how to involve them in your daily activities. Of course you also need to schedule real play time at set times with Mom or Dad when your kids can have all your attention.

- Small children demand a lot of attention. Sometimes it seems you can't take your eyes off of them or that they can't amuse themselves alone. With the games in this book, they'll often be occupied for a long time. There are also games in which you can involve brothers, sisters, or other children.

- Safety comes first! Watch out for sharp edges or small objects that can disappear in the mouth. Provide play cloths that can easily washed when things get messy.

1 player

at least 2 players

several players

with adult

0 - 18
months

The Moon is Round

0-18 months

- Place your baby on his back. Using your finger, draw a round face on his belly.
- Say or sing the following verse: "The moon is round. It has two eyes, a nose, and a mouth."

Things you'll need:

- a soft place to lie down (bed, couch, blanket, etc.)

Did you know that...

- There are a lot of variations on verses and rhymes–read nursery rhyme books together to find ones that your child likes and that can have actions to perform as you say the verse.
- Little children like it when you sing a song for them and hug and tickle them while changing them or giving them a bath.
- You can make up your own version. Your baby will soon recognize it.

0-18 months

Peekaboo

Things you'll need:

- if desired, a wall, book, or blanket to hide yourself

- Sit down in front of your baby and make sure he can watch you closely.
- Put your hands in front of your face.
- Open your hands and say "Peekaboo!"
- Repeat this as long as you see he likes the game. You can also hide yourself behind a large object.

Did you know that...

- Part of infant development is learning that objects or people still exist even when they are hidden.
- Babies from about six months notice when the person who takes care of them leaves–this provokes feelings of fear and sadness.
- By playing Peekaboo, you can teach children that somebody who leaves also comes back.

Grasping Hands

0-18 months

- Put your baby on his back.
- Hold out your two forefingers to him. You'll feel that he grasps your fingers tightly.
- Pulling slowly, you can pull him up. Even newborns can grasp tightly and will try to hold their heads upright.

Things you'll need:

- a soft place to lie down (bed, couch, blanket, etc.)

0-18 months

Search for the Sound

Things you'll need:

- toys which make sounds

- Put your baby in a spot where he can easily look around him.
- Stand in front of him and make a noise with the toy. When he notices the sound and looks at you, you can stand a bit further away. He'll be fascinated by the sound and keeping searching for its origin.

Baby on the Belly

0-18 months

- Lie down on your back and put your baby belly-down on your belly.
- Hold your baby tight and caress his back.

Things you'll need:

- a soft place to lie down (bed, couch, blanket, etc.)

Did you know that...

- Babies like to be snuggled close to those who take care of them.
- They feel protected and learn that the world is a safe place where they will be cared for. This gives them a feeling of trust that they'll carry with them their whole lives.

0-18 months

Roll Over

Things you'll need:

- a soft place to lie down (bed, couch, blanket, etc.)

- Put your baby on his belly and push him softly on his side.
- When he's ready for it (about seven months), he'll roll on his back and back again.
- After a while he'll do this all alone.

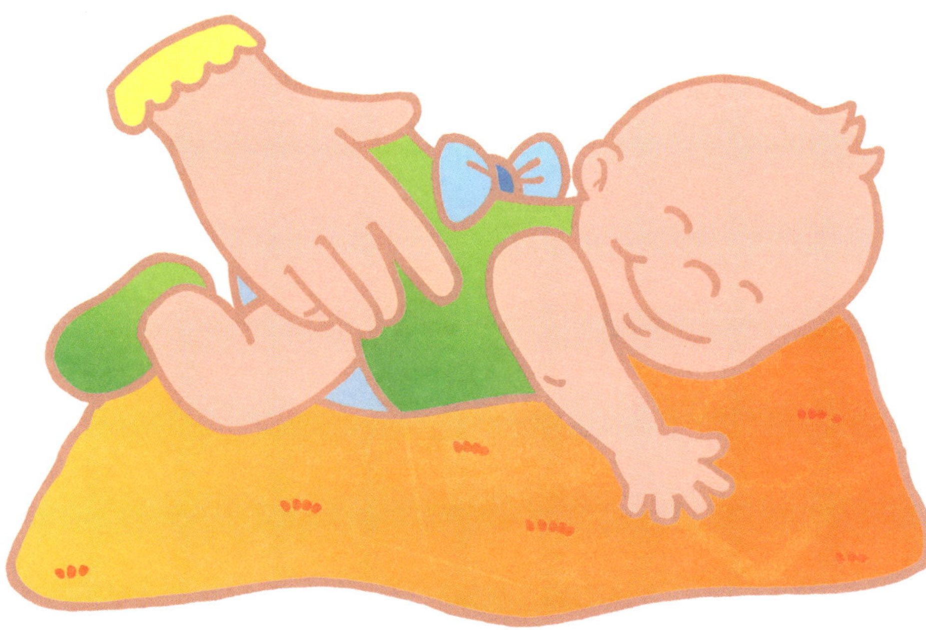

Did you know that...

- Around four to five months babies learn to control their movements.
- Their bodies become strong enough to hold their heads up. They can roll over and sit up all alone.

Touch and Feel Books

0-18 months

- Cut cardboard or paper squares of the same size.
- Use the glue to attach different materials on each page: floppy bits of yarn, soft cotton balls, shiny foil, etc.
- Make a hole in the left upper corner of each square and tie a ribbon through it.
- You have now a touch and feel book in which different materials can be discovered in a fun way. You can change the book endlessly.

Things you'll need:

- stiff paper or cardboard, colored if desired
- a hole punch
- a ribbon
- glue
- cotton balls
- yarn
- aluminum foil

Did you know that...

- Children in their first months discover life around them by their senses.
- Through their skin they are in contact with the world. They enjoy especially soft materials.
- Until their second birthday most children continue to rely on their mouths as the primary way to experience an object. They'll love to put new toys in their mouths. If you want, you can laminate the pages to make the book waterproof.

0-18 months

Red and Round

Things you'll need:

- a red balloon
- a string

- Blow up the balloon and tie it with the string over the baby's crib or play yard.
- Your baby will be fascinated with the big red round object!

Did you know that...

- Babies like big and round objects.
- They are also fascinated by human faces. They love to watch the faces of Mom or Dad and to touch them.

In the Air

0-18 months

- Lie on your back and hold your baby horizontal with your two hands. Do this only when he can hold his head up and when his back is strong enough.
- Stretch your arms so you can lift your baby up in the air. Move him around so it looks like your baby is flying. You'll see he will crow with pleasure!

Things you'll need:

- a soft place to lie down (bed, couch, blanket, etc.)

0-18 months

Colored Rattle

Things you'll need:

- a plastic bottle, when possible in a bright color
- pasta in different shapes, like macaroni
- rice

- Fill the bottle with the macaroni and/or rice.
- Tighten the cap.
- You have a rattle which your baby can use to make noise!

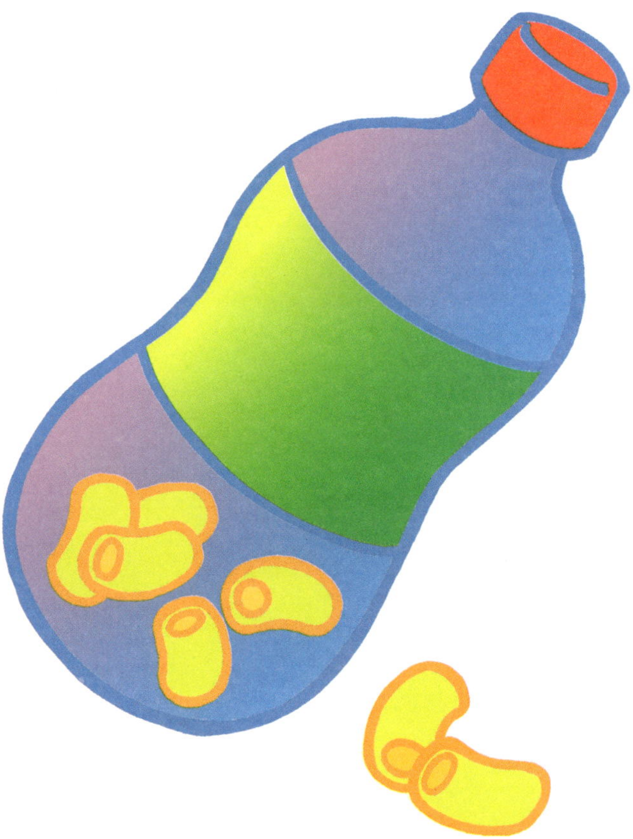

In the Bath

0-18 months

- Fill the bottom of the bath with tepid water.
- Put your baby in the bath and give him the plastic jars and toys.
- While you wash him, he'll have fun scooping the water or sailing the boats.

Things you'll need:

- a bathtub
- plastic jars and bottles
- plastic toys
- a sponge, a soft brush

Did you know that...

- Often babies like to be bathed.
- They like it when you tell them what you're doing as you wash them and take care of them. They feel comfortable being naked in the water.

0-18 months

On the Trampoline

Things you'll need:

- a soft place to lie down (bed, couch, blanket, etc.)

- Lie on your back and put your baby on your belly while you hold him tightly. Do this activity only when he can hold up his head and when his back is strong enough.
- Stretch your arms so you lift your child up in the air and then let him land softly on your belly.
- You'll notice that your child will soon position his legs so it looks like he is jumping on a trampoline.

Grabbing Feet

0-18 months

- Put your baby on his back and press gently against the ball of his foot.
- This will make him curl his toes as though he wants to grab something. This curling of his toes also happens when the ball of his foot touches the floor and he may make a stepping motion.

Things you'll need:

- a soft place to lie down (bed, couch, blanket, etc.)

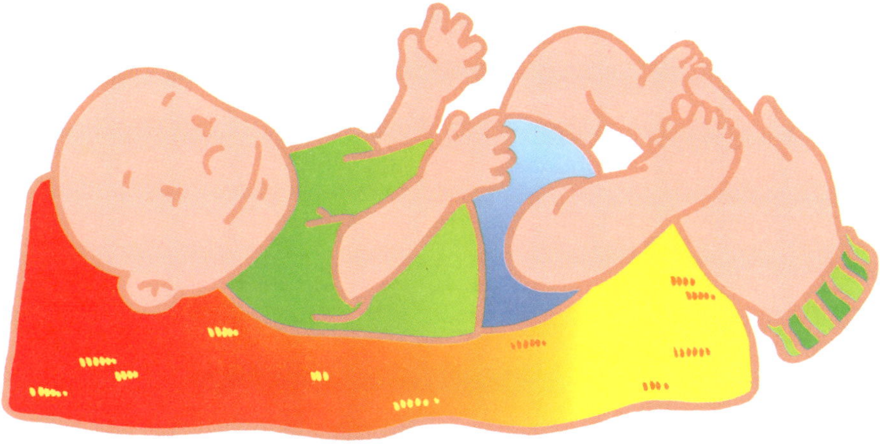

Did you know that...

- Babies have a lot of primitive and survival reflexes in their first months.
- The Babinski toe curling reflex is one example–other reflexes are rooting and sucking when an object touches their cheeks or mouths..
- These reflexes disappear after a while. Around eight months a child will keep his foot flexed when you push on the ball of his foot.

0-18 months

Reading a Book

Things you'll need:

- cardboard books with vivid colored drawings or pictures

- Hold your child on your lap and let him pick a book.
- Read the book or explain the story. Maybe he can identify what's in the pictures!

Did you know that...

- Reading books together is very good for children.
- It's not only a way to be close to your child but it also helps him to learn language.
- You can do this as a ritual–for instance, before going to sleep.

Hide-and-Seek

0-18 months

- Play together with the toy.
- Make sure he watches the toy and hide it under a blanket.
- Your child will search for the toy.

Things you'll need:

- a toy
- a blanket or a sheet

Climbing

Things you'll need:

- a soft place to kneel

- Kneel on your knees in front of your child.
- Let him step with one foot on one of your knees, and then his other foot can step on your other knee, next on your thighs, and so on. Meanwhile, hold him tightly.
- When he has is climbed all the way up you, you can give him a big hug!

Did you know that...

- Kids from eight months learn to walk holding a hand of an adult.
- They learn to pull themselves up on furniture.
- Their first steps are about thirteen months.

Magic Bubbles

0-18 months

- Blow bubbles with the suds.
- Your baby will love to help and will be fascinated with those magic bubbles in beautiful colors.

Things you'll need:

- a bucket with soapsuds
- a bubble blowing wand

0-18 months

Tug-of-War

Things you'll need:

- a soft place for your baby to sit
- an old scarf

- Make sure your baby sits firmly on a cushioned surface. Give him an end of the scarf and hold the other end yourself.
- Pull gently on the scarf so your child notices the movement. Encourage him to pull also.
- Who is the strongest?

Little Drummer

0-18 months

- Put all the buckets, blocks, and boxes next to each other.
- Tap out different rhythms with your hands. Your baby will love to imitate you and make music himself!

Things you'll need:

- plastic buckets
- wooden blocks and boxes

Finger Faces

0-18 months

Things you'll need:

- colored pens or markers

- Draw a face on your fingertip. This fingertip can move and talk to the baby.
- Using faces you draw on your other fingers you can act out a story.

Foam Funnies

0-18 months

- With suds you can make a hat, a beard, or any silly thing on yourself.
- Your baby will notice that you look different and will probably laugh at your funny look.

Things you'll need:

- soapsuds

Did you know that...

- You can involve a child in all the aspects of your daily life.
- Bring your baby into the bathroom with you as you get ready in the morning. Find a safe place for him to sit or lie and watch you.

0-18 months

A Watering Can

Things you'll need:

- a plastic bottle
- a knife
- water
- sand

- Make holes with a knife in the bottom of a bottle.
- Fill the bottle with the water and hold it over a bowl or sink. Your baby will watch amazed at how the water seeps through.
- You can also dribble water into a tub of sand. Your baby will like to feel it!

Air Soccer

0-18 months

- Sit down in front of your child. Put a ping-pong ball on the floor in front of you and blow it to him.
- Maybe he'll try to grab the ball. Maybe you can show him how to move it by blowing against it!

Things you'll need:

- ping-pong balls

0-18 months

Hungry Lions

Things you'll need:

- a knife
- a cardboard box
- paint or markers
- yarn
- soft balls

- Cut out a big hole in one side of the cardboard box. Paint or draw a lion's head around the hole. Decorate it with yarn.
- Put your child in front of the box and give him a soft ball. Can he throw it in the lion's jaws?

Did you know that...

- Children at about thirteen months can pick up an object and throw it.
- From that age on they'll become more dexterous and independent. For instance, they like to put on or pull off their socks themselves.

Cream Paintings

0-18 months

- Place your child at the table or on the ground before the tray.
- Put a bit of whipped cream on the tray and let the baby put his hands in it. He can paint with the whipped cream or just feel the fun texture.

Things you'll need:

- whipped cream
- a large tray

0-18 months

Obstacle Course

Things you'll need:

- a soft surface
- chairs
- cardboard boxes
- wooden blocks

- As soon as a child can walk, he likes to discover the world around him. Make an obstacle course for him with chairs to walk around and climb over or boxes to crawl through.
- At the end he'll find a reward: his favorite toy, a yummy treat, or a hug.

Pushing

0-18 months

- Give your child a box, tub, or basket he can push while walking.
- Everything else will have to move aside!

Things you'll need:

- a cardboard box, a tub, or laundry basket

Did you know that...

- Little walkers often like to push things.
- They can use their strollers or bikes but also big boxes and tubs.
- Stay close to prevent accidents.

0-18 months

Paper Shredding

Things you'll need:

- old paper (magazines, newspapers, etc.)

- Give your child an old magazine or newspaper.
- He'll remain happy for a long time tearing apart the paper or making balls of paper.
- Stay around to make sure that no balls of paper disappear into the mouth!

Finger Puppets

0-18 months

- Cut out a piece of cloth double the size of a fingertip.
- Fold it double and sew it together so it fits on the fingertip-either your fingertip or your child's.
- With the felt-tip pen or the needle and thread you can give it a face or other details to make it a finger puppet.

Things you'll need:

- a piece of scrap cloth
- a pair of scissors
- needle and thread
- a felt-tip pen

0-18 months

Telephone

Things you'll need:

- an old telephone, disconnected

- Give your child an old telephone.
- He'll like to push the buttons, but he'll also use it to talk to you. It'll be extra fun when you play along with your telephone.

Did you know that...

- Children from about one year start to speak words.
- By using one word, they can soon make their meanings clear, like "Look!" or "Coat!"
- They'll also like to imitate adults and babble whole stories.

18-36 months

Building a Skyscraper

18-36 months

- Put all the boxes, jars, and blocks together. Take one and put another on top of it.
- Your toddler can finish the tower. How high will this skyscraper become?

Things you'll need:

- boxes
- plastic jars with flat surfaces or clean food containers
- blocks

Did you know that...

- Toddlers are fascinated by piling boxes on top of each other and building towers.
- They'll be interested by pots and boxes that stack. But they'll also enjoy knocking down the tower!

18-36 months

Cardboard House

Things you'll need:

- a large cardboard box

- Choose a cardboard box that is big enough so your child fits in it completely.
- You can turn it into a small house by cutting out a door or by decorating the walls.

Swinging

18-36 months

- Hold the blanket or the towel together with another adult so your toddler can lie down on it.
- Raise the blanket and swing it gently so you rock your toddler back and forth.

Things you'll need:

- a large towel or a blanket

Did you know that...

- Swinging movements have a relaxing effect on children.
- You can do this activity before going to sleep but also as a fun game anytime!

18-36 months

Filling and Dumping

Things you'll need:

- plastic jars or cups
- large beads or blocks

- The jars and cups can be filled by the beads and the blocks.
- The contents can also be poured from one cup into the other.

Did you know that...

- Toddlers search for things that fit in each other.
- They like to fill cups and jars and then dump them out. Be careful about little objects disappearing in their mouths!

Ball Pit

18-36 months

- Fill the laundry basket or box half full with the balls. Put your child in the middle of them.
- Your toddler can feel the balls on his skin, especially if he's not wearing lots of layers of clothes. You can also use a ball to stroke his legs, arms, feet, etc. Let it "rain" balls all over his body.

Things you'll need:

- a large laundry basket or box
- several small and large balls (tennis balls, beanbags, ping-pong balls ...)

Did you know that...

- Children learn materials by feeling them.
- With a "feeling game" you stimulate the sense of touch and also relax the skin.

18-36 months

Driving

Things you'll need:

- a large laundry basket or box

- Place the laundry basket or box on the ground and let your toddler crawl in it.
- Push the basket or box around like a car. Your toddler can make the "vroom" noises.

Mirror Mirror

18-36 months

- Put a red dot with the finger-paint on the nose of your toddler.
- Does he realize who the funny clown in the mirror is?

Things you'll need:

- a mirror
- red finger-paint

Did you know that...

- Toddlers from about twenty months understand that a mirror shows the reflection of reality.
- From that moment they stop looking for the child behind the mirror.

18-36 months

Who Has the Block?

Things you'll need:

- a small object (for example, a block)

- Pass the block from hand to hand among several people.
- Can your toddler guess who has the block?

Sand and Water

18-36 months

- Your toddler can play in the sand with the water and the jars and bottles.
- He'll soon discover that the water changes the sand.

Things you'll need:

- a sandbox outside
- sand
- bottles and jars filled with water

Did you know that...

- You don't have to have a sandbox in your yard to let your child play with sand.
- Many playgrounds have areas where your child can play with sand. Of course you can also make a trip to the beach and have fun!

18-36 months

Things on the Slide

Things you'll need:

- a wooden shelf or board
- small objects

- Put the wooden board at an angle against the couch or table to create a slide that things can roll down.
- Maybe the slide is big and strong enough for your toddler slide down as well.

Hanging Orchestra

18-36 months

- Tie all the objects on the rope. Tie the rope to a clothesline or fence and let the objects hang down where your child can reach them.
- Give your child a wooden spoon or stick and let him make music with the objects.

Things you'll need:

- cans, plastic pots, bottles, pans
- rope
- a wooden spoon or stick
- a clothesline or a fence

18-36 months

Toddler's Gym

Things you'll need:

- a chair
- a broomstick

- The chair can be used to crawl underneath.
- The broomstick becomes a horizontal bar when adults hold the ends. Your toddler can hold onto the bar and try to lift himself.

Did you know that...

- Toddlers from about nineteen months become real acrobats.
- They can climb, hang, or ride on a rocking horse. All objects they find in the house are inspiring. They'll have their own ideas about crawling through a fallen chair or to pulling it behind them.

Heaven in the Laundry

18-36 months

- Your toddler can crawl in the laundry basket.
- It's nice and soft on top, between, or under the clothes, sheets, and towels.

Things you'll need:

- a laundry basket with clothes, sheets, or towels

Did you know that...

- Toddlers prefer to play with adults nearby.
- This doesn't mean you have to play with your toddler all the time, but you can incorporate his play into your daily tasks.

18-36 months

Jumping Safely

Things you'll need:

- a soft surface with sheets, pillows, and blankets
- a high object (for example, a chair)

- Let your toddler stand on the chair and jump down onto the soft surface.
- When he is scared, you can help him, of course. He'll also love to jump into the arms of a confident person.

Did you know that...

- Toddlers experience jumping as flying.
- Often they can estimate instinctively whether a height is dangerous for them. However, it's advisable to keep an eye on them!

Pillow Fight

18-36 months

- Kneel on the ground and hold a pillow in front of you.
- Your toddler stands in front of you with his pillow.
- Push the pillows against each other gently. Who will topple over first?

Things you'll need:

- a soft surface with sheets, pillows, and blankets
- pillows

One, Two, Hop!

18-36 months

A lifting game

- The toddler walks hand-in-hand between you and another adult.
- Hold his wrists tightly and lift him after saying, "one, two, hop!" Walking together becomes fun!

Giddy up!

18-36 months

- Your toddler will love pretending you're his horse and riding on your back as you crawl on your hands and knees. You can also give him rides when you are sitting down by bouncing him on your knees.

A lifting game

Toddler's Dance

18-36 months

Things you'll need:

- a music player
- cheerful music

- With all furniture moved aside any room becomes a real dance floor.
- Exciting music will make your toddler want to dance.

Fingerprints

18-36 months

- Your toddler can draw alone using his fingers.
- He'll learn that his fingertip leaves a mark and that way he can draw lines.

Things you'll need:

- finger-paint
- a washable surface
- paper

Puzzle of Pictures

18-36 months

Things you'll need:

- colorful pictures
- a pair of scissors
- thick cardboard
- glue

- Glue a picture on the cardboard.
- Cut in into two (four at the most) pieces so it becomes a puzzle. Your toddler can try to fit the pieces together.

Did you know that...

- Toddlers are fascinated by puzzles of all kind.
- They like to figure out how everything fits and to name everything they see. When they put the puzzle together and a picture of themselves or a brother or sister appears, they'll certainly be delighted.

Animals Everywhere

18-36 months

- Little children are fascinated by animals.
- Show your toddler the animals in your neighborhood, like birds, squirrels, or rabbits. Or take him to a farm or a fair to see sheep and goats. He'll also like an excursion to the zoo!

Setting out!

18-36 months

Carwash

Things you'll need:

- a little bucket with soapsuds
- a little sponge
- a little watering can

- With the bucket and the sponge your toddler can help wash the car.
- The soapsuds can be washed away by the watering can.

Did you know that...

- For playing you don't need always toys.
- Toddlers learn to discover their world and prefer to do this through familiar people like their parents or grandparents.
- Toddlers imitate as a natural developmental stage. They like to copy adults, especially in everyday tasks. So give your toddler a small dustpan and brush because he would love to help you with the house cleaning!

House Painting

18-36 months

- With the old paintbrush your toddler can "paint" the outside walls of the house with water. It'll be very exciting for him when the sun dries the "paint."

Things you'll need:

- a small bucket with water
- an old paintbrush

18-36 months

Catch Me If You Can

A hug game

- Give your child a head start running and then try to catch up with him.
- When you catch up, you have to give him a big hug, of course!

I Spy!

18-36 months

- Decorate the toilet paper tubes with vivid colors. Tape the tubes together to make binoculars.
- With these binoculars your toddler can go on a voyage of discovery–what will he see?

Things you'll need:

- two toilet paper tubes
- felt-tip pens or paint
- tape

18-36 months

Kitchen Helper

Things you'll need:

- pots and pans
- a wooden spoon

- While you are cooking, your toddler can stir in his own pot.
- Maybe there are other ways you can find for him to help as well?

Memory

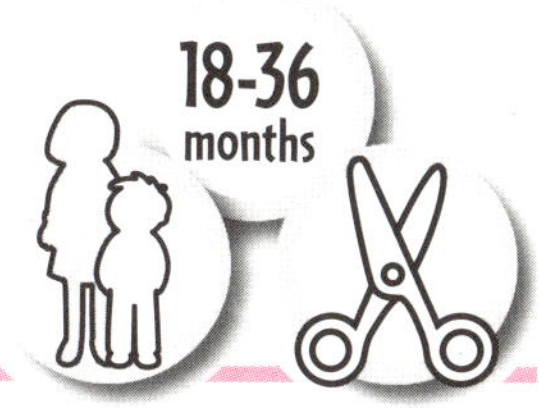

- Glue the pictures on the cardboard. Cut them out in equal size squares.
- Put the cards down on the table with the backside up.
- Your toddler can turn over two pictures at the same time and try to guess where the two matching pictures are.

Things you'll need:

- pairs of pictures
- cardboard
- a pair of scissors
- glue

18-36 months

Finish the Song

A language game

- Sing your child's favorite song.
- If you stop before the end, can he say or sing the next words?

Sidewalk Artist

18-36 months

- Your toddler can make drawings on the sidewalk with the chalk.
- What pictures can he make?

Things you'll need:

- colored chalk

18-36 months

Indoor Camping

Things you'll need:

- a sheet or a blanket
- a table
- chairs

- Hang the sheet over the table so you create a cozy covered spot under the table. Or you can hang the sheet over the chairs to make a tent.
- This tent might become your toddler's favorite spot which he can equip as he wants with his favorite toys.
- In good weather you can also make a tent in the yard.

3 - 4
years

Catching Balls

3-4 years

- Have all the children stand in a row.
- Stand in front of them and take turns throwing the ball to each child.
- Who can catch the ball?

Things you'll need:

- a little ball

3-4 years

Candy Memory

Things you'll need:

- ten cups
- five pairs of the same candies

- Spread the candies over the table. Place a cup over each candy.
- Each child can take turns lifting two cups, looking for two of the same candies.
- When they find a pair of candies, they can eat them as a reward!

Musical Newspapers

3-4 years

- Put the same number of pieces of newspaper on the ground as the number of children there are.
- Start the music and let the children walk between the newspapers. When the music stops, they have to find a piece of newspaper to stand on.
- As soon as the music starts, take one newspaper away. The one who isn't standing on a piece of newspaper when the music stops is out.
- Who will be the last one?

Things you'll need:

- a pile of newspapers
- a music player
- music

Picture Box

Things you'll need:

- a shoebox
- old magazines
- glue
- a pair of scissors

- Cut two holes in the short side of the shoebox– these will be the viewing holes.
- Select pictures with a certain theme. For example, pictures of animals if you have just visited a farm or zoo.
- Glue the pictures inside and outside the box.
- Through the viewing holes your tiny tot can admire a world of animals!

Did you know that...

- Going to pre-school can be a complete change for many children.
- You can prepare them for this step by looking together for pictures of classes of children or school scenes.

Sand Doughnut Holes

3-4 years

- Make round balls of sand. Some extra water can help.
- The balls can go in the bucket to be fried into doughnut holes.
- With a sieve and some dry sand, "sugar" can be poured over the balls.

Things you'll need:

- sand
- water
- a bucket, scoops, sieves, etc.

Did you know that...

- Children have a rich fantasy life.
- A cardboard box becomes a castle and a sandbox a doughnut bakery.
- Let them play and fantasize. You'll be surprised at the worlds they can create for themselves.

Like the Grown-ups

3-4 years

Things you'll need:

- a storage box
- old clothes
- old accessories, like eye glasses, cooking utensils, purses, etc.

- Fill a box with old things and clothes.
- This will be the box where your child can dig around as much as he wants to to play "like the grown-ups." With the glasses on his nose, he's Dad reading the newspaper, with the cooking utensils, he can be Mom working in the kitchen.

Did you know that...

- Children are very observant of the world around them.
- They watch what adults do very closely and love to imitate what they see. This is how they process the information they pick up during the day.

Picasso Junior

3-4 years

- With the pencils the tiny tot can draw enthusiastically.
- Will he become a Picasso?

Things you'll need:

- paper
- pencils

Did you know that...

- Learning to draw goes step by step.
- Children mostly start by making marks on the paper. From three years old, they start to make shapes.
- The circle is the first shape that children recognize. After all, it looks like the thing that is most interesting to them–the face.
- Gradually they'll draw limbs, but not a body. You'll see many heads with just feet or heads with arms and legs.

3-4 years

Sorting Colors

Things you'll need:

- different objects, many with the same colors

- Put all the objects together in a pile. Can your tiny tot name all the colors and place the objects with the same color together?
- You can help him by starting a pile for each color.

Did you know that...

- Children are fascinated by colors.
- From about the age of two years they learn to recognize and name colors. Later they are able to group and classify them.

Puppet Show

3-4 years

- You don't need to pay a lot for a puppet theater. You can make one yourself. You can use your child's dolls or stuffed animals. You also can buy simple and cheap puppets.
- Cut a large square in the long side of the cardboard box. Make a hole in both short sides.
- Look for pictures for your background scenery in magazines. Decorate the inside of the box with the pictures. Close the top of the box and decorate the outside with nice colors.
- Hang the tablecloth over the ironing board or the table and put your puppet theater on top of it. Place the open front side forwards and put your arms with the puppets through the holes at the sides of the box. Now you can bring the puppet show to life!

Things you'll need:

- a cardboard box
- a pair of scissors
- glue
- old magazines
- a tablecloth
- an ironing board or a table
- puppets

Did you know that...

- Tiny tots adore puppet shows.
- They like to create a whole world with their stories.
- With this puppet theater, not only do you get to have fun together making it, but you or your kids will also get to perform a show. With an audience it's extra fun!

3-4 years

Pyramid

Things you'll need:

- about ten plastic pots or blocks
- a little ball

- Build a pyramid with the objects.
- Who can knock over the pyramid with the ball?

Did you know that...

- Children from the age of three become more and more dexterous.
- They can more easily manage fine materials and small objects and they can throw at a target with better aim. Their fine motor skills are advancing.

Newspaper Maze

3-4 years

- Place the chairs and the tables near each other.
- Hang the newspapers over each chair and table to create passages to crawl through. Arrange these passages so you create a maze your child can crawl through.

Things you'll need:

- chairs
- tables
- newspapers

3-4 years

Slalom

Things you'll need:

- yogurt containers or blocks

- Place the containers at a short distance from each other.
- The tiny tot has to walk around the containers, zigzagging back and forth.
- If he knocks down a container, he has to put it back in line.

Did you know that...

- From the moment children can walk, they like to practice walking and play walking games.
- Slalom walking, hopping, or jumping are things they will find fun and challenging.
- Endless variations on these run and jump games exist. You can use your imagination to improve the walking and running skills of your tiny tot.

Self-portrait

3-4 years

- Put the paper on the ground. Make sure the paper is as large as your child.
- If necessary, tape several pieces of paper to each other.
- Let your child lie down on the paper and trace his body on the paper.
- He can color in this drawing. Of course, you can help him!
- Now he has a life-sized portrait of himself.

Things you'll need:

- large paper (packing paper, poster board, old wallpaper, etc.)
- colored pencils or felt-tip pens
- tape

3-4 years

Limbo

Things you'll need:

- a long scarf

- Two adults hold the ends of the scarf at the child's height. Your tiny tot can easily walk under it.
- Every time your child walks under the scarf, you hold it a bit lower. How low can he go?

Playing Store

3-4 years

- Today your tiny tot can play store!
- On the table he can arrange the boxes and the cans to make a real store display.
- Another table can be the counter with the plastic tray as a cash register. "Customers" can pay with play money.

Things you'll need:

- empty boxes and cans of food
- tables
- a plastic tray
- play money, if desired

Did you know that...

- Children like to copy daily life.
- They can amuse themselves for a long time by playing store or hospital.

3-4 years

Jumping for Soap Bubbles

Things you'll need:

- a bubble blowing wand
- soapsuds

- Your tiny tot can jump to catch the bubbles you blow.
- Can he catch them with his hands? Maybe he can also blow bubbles?

Walking a Tightrope

3-4 years

- Put the rope on the ground.
- Can your child walk on it? It'll be even more fun when you arrange the rope in waves and squiggles.

Things you'll need:

- a thick rope

Did you know that...

- Children from the age of three can play alone easily.
- This is because of their curiosity and their brain development.
- However, they often cannot stay focused on one game very long. So it's normal when your child is playing a game one moment and is looking for another adventure the next moment.

Statues

3-4 years

Things you'll need:

- a music player
- music

- Start the music. Your child can start dancing and walking around.
- At the moment that the music stops, he has to stand still.
- How long can he hold still? Any means can be employed to get him to move: tickling and giggling is allowed!

Monkey See, Monkey Do

3-4 years

- Sit down in front of your tiny tot and make silly faces.
- Your child has to try to imitate all your faces and gestures. Who will laugh first?

Imitation game

Dance of the Toys

Things you'll need:

- a music player
- music
- stuffed animals and dolls

- Move all the chairs and tables aside and put on a happy song.
- Your tiny tot can dance together with his animals and dolls.

Did you know that...

- Children are very attached to their stuffed animals and dolls.
- These are comforting objects for them which can make them feel safe at difficult moments.
- It doesn't have to be the most beautiful toy from the store. Children can also be attached to their baby blankets.

Big and Little Waves

3-4 years

- Take the towel on one side and give the other end to your tiny tot.
- By waving your arms softly up and down you can make waves in the towel. Your little friend would love to join.

Things you'll need:

- **towels or blankets**

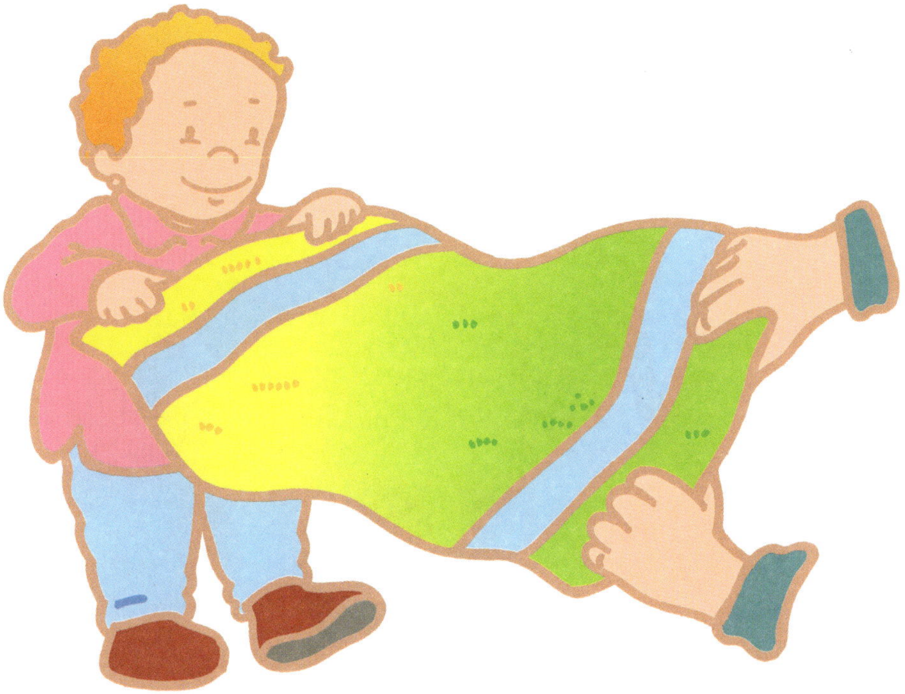

Did you know that...

- Children from the age of three slowly start to realize that what they do has consequences.
- They learn, for example, that they can turn off the light by moving the switch or that they can make waves in the towel by moving their arms.
- Life is starting to become predictable for them, and they are beginning to learn how they play a part.

3-4 years

Preschool Bowling

Things you'll need:

- plastic bottles
- a little ball

- Arrange the bottles in a triangle.
- From a few steps back your tiny tot can try to knock over the bottles by rolling the ball. Who can do the best?

Throwing Stones

3-4 years

- Draw a line on the ground with the stick. Everybody stands behind this line.
- Take the colored stone and throw it a little ways.
- Everybody can take turns trying to throw a stone as close as possible to the colored stone.
- When everybody has tried, you can look to see who was the closest. That person wins.

Things you'll need:

- stones of a different size
- one colored stone
- a flat surface in the yard
- a stick

3-4 years

Paper Hat

Things you'll need:

- an old newspaper

- Take a page of the newspaper and fold it in half horizontally. Fold this again in half horizontally and then open it so you have a vertical line.
- Take the left upper corner and fold it down to the vertical line. Do the same with the right upper corner.
- Fold the first strip under the triangle up. Turn the whole thing over and fold the back strip up as well.
- Now you have a paper hat for your little one!

Hello? Hello?

3-4 years

- Make a hole in the bottom of the cups.
- Put the rope through the holes and make a knot in the rope in the inside of the cups.
- When you pull the rope tightly, you can talk into the cups and listen.

Things you'll need:

- two cardboard cups
- a piece of rope
- a pair of scissors

3-4 years

Musical Legs

Things you'll need:

- toilet paper tubes
- rice, pasta, or dried corn
- colored paper
- a pair of scissors
- glue
- rope

- Draw two circles on the colored paper, cut them out and glue one on the opening of the toilet paper tube.
- Fill the toilet paper tube with rice, pasta, or corn. Glue the second circle on the other opening and decorate the rest of the tube.
- You can tie these "maracas" on your child's legs with the rope. This will give your child a musical walk!

Basketball

3-4 years

- Make a circle in front of you with your arms.
- Your child has to try to throw the ball or the socks in the "basket."
- You can make the game easy in the beginning by bending down. Then you can make it more difficult by holding the "basket" higher each time.

Things you'll need:

- a ball of yarn or rolled up socks

3-4 years

Underwater Spyglass

Things you'll need:

- a plastic bucket or cup
- a knife
- plastic cling wrap
- a rubber band

- With the knife cut out the bottom of the bucket or cup.
- Stretch the cling wrap over the opening and hold it in place with the rubber band.
- Now you have a spyglass which your child can use to discover things underwater.

4 - 5 years

Decorating Faces

4-5 years

- Tear out pictures of people in magazines.
- Your pre-schooler can enjoy himself by decorating these pictures. The lovely lady gets a pimple on her nose. The distinguished gentleman gets a stubbly beard and an earring.

Things you'll need:

- **old magazines**
- **felt-tip pens, crayons**

Did you know that...

- Pre-schoolers know very well the difference between "good" and "bad."
- This understanding begins from the second year of life and will be more developed through the years. You can help their learning by indicating clearly what's ok and what not. Jumping on the couch can be punished by a look and a word, while sitting neatly at the table gets rewarded with a loving touch on the head.
- At the age of four years children can make the distinction between things they can't do and things they can do under certain circumstances. They can have fun decorating the magazine pictures under the approving eye of Mom or Dad, but they'll know that this activity isn't allowed on the pictures in the family album.

4-5 years

Sticking Raisins

Things you'll need:

- a plate with raisins
- toothpicks

- Put the plate with the raisins and the toothpicks on the table.
- Stick a raisin on a toothpick. Now you can stick another toothpick into this raisin.
- You can stick several toothpicks to each other and make a house or a doll.
- Keep enough raisins so your child can eat some, too. Take care he doesn't poke himself with the sharp tips of the toothpicks.

Tastes Differ

4-5 years

- With this game your pre-schooler can taste lots of different things but it'll be a blind taste test!
- Blindfold the pre-schooler with the scarf and let him taste from all the bowls and glasses one by one. Can he guess which treat it is?

Things you'll need:

- a scarf
- bowls filled with different food: pudding, apple slices, grapes, chocolate, etc.
- glasses filled with different drinks: apple juice, milk, water, etc.

Did you know that...

- Pre-schoolers from this age on can distinguish tastes and smells?
- They develop their own flavor preferences. That's why they won't be always happy when Brussels sprouts are on the menu!

4-5 years

What's That Smell?

Things you'll need:

- plastic pots or bowls
- things that smell

- Search for smells in the house, garden, or garage.
- Mom's perfume can be "caught" by sprinkling a bit on a handkerchief. Fresh mown grass or just baked bread has an odor, too. You can "catch" those smells by putting some of the grass or bread in a pot.
- Play a game with these smells: can your child guess what's in the pots?

Did you know that...

- The smell is the least developed sense.
- For that reason it's good to help little ones get confident with these odors and to let them name the smells.

Predicting

4-5 years

- Somebody starts to make a drawing. After each line or shape he stops for a while.
- Can the others predict what he's drawing?

Things you'll need:

- paper
- a pencil

4-5 years

Sea Game

Things you'll need:

- 4 branches
- 3 shells
- 3 stones

- Use the four branches to make a game board with nine squares–place two branches horizontally and two vertically.
- Everybody takes turns putting one shell or stone in one of the squares. Can somebody make three shells or three stones in a row?

Did you know that...

- Children love lakes and oceans.
- It's a favorite vacation spot for most families because you have so many play opportunities for the children. They can horse around all they want!

Riddle Game

4-5 years

Language game

- Think up riddles about animals, objects, or people your pre-schooler knows. For example: I'm tall, my hide is gray, and I have a long trunk. Who am I?
- You can also consider this as a way to bring back memories. For example: We drove a long time that day, you were bored in the back of the car, and you wanted to see the large animals first. Can your pre-schooler guess which memory you're talking about?

Did you know that...

- Children have to process a lot of new things in their lives.
- You can help them best by talking a lot about those things and naming the feelings they had. Even though your child doesn't understand everything you say, he'll certainly understand the intonation in your voice.

Tin Can Stilts

4-5 years

Things you'll need:

- two empty cans
- a knife or can opener
- two pieces of strong rope

- For each can, turn the can upside-down and make two holes, one on each side of the can, close to the bottom of the can. Pull the rope through the holes and make a knot inside the can.
- Make sure you make two rope loops of the same length. Take into account the height of your child. Standing on the cans he has to be able to hold the loops.
- Your pre-schooler can try to walk on the cans.

Treasure Hunt

4-5 years

- The children close their eyes while you hide the plastic bag of candy in the sand.
- Then they can walk around to look for the treasure. You can say "warm" or "cold" when they are close or far.
- Whoever finds the treasure can distribute the candy!

Things you'll need:

- a beach or a sandbox
- a shovel
- a plastic bag with candy

4-5 years

Pre-school Rap

Language game

- Somebody says a sentence. For example: "Today we visited the zoo." The next person has to say something that rhymes. For example: "And we ate ice cream, too." The next person continues. When there are just two people, you can alternate.

- When you can't make up something, you can repeat the last sentence. The idea is that there is no silence. Together you'll make a nice rap song.

Did you know that...

- Most children from this age speak their native language fluently.
- You can occupy children for a long time and everywhere with language games. Even when they don't succeed every time, they like to be challenged to talk correctly.

Forbidden to Laugh

4-5 years

Giggle game

- In this game it's forbidden to laugh!
- You can make the game more difficult by tickling each other or making silly faces. Whoever laughs first has to do a crazy punishment, like painting red dots on his face or putting his coat on backwards.

Marble Darts

4-5 years

Things you'll need:

- a beach or a sandbox
- a branch
- marbles or rocks

- Using the branch, draw five circles around each other. In the inner circle you write a 5, in the next a 4, etc. Now you have a "dartboard" in the sand.
- Step away a couple of steps from the dartboard and draw a line. You have to throw your marbles or stones from this line.
- Try to aim toward the middle because that gives you the most points. Who will become the darts champion?

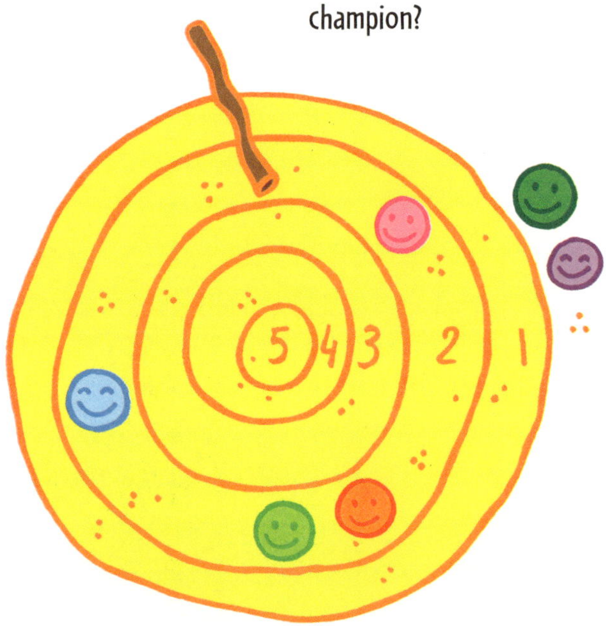

Did you know that...

- Children from pre-school age learn to make rules and they will stick to them.
- When playing party games your child learns to consider others. He learns to wait his turn, to work together, and to lose.

Half Pictures

4-5 years

- Draw a line down the middle of the back of the pictures. Your child can neatly cut the picture in half using this line.
- You get a series of half pictures you can mix up.
- Now your child needs to look for matching pictures. Or maybe he can make fun combinations of uncle and grandma!

Things you'll need:

- old pictures
- a pair of scissors
- a ruler
- a pencil

Balloon Pass

4-5 years

Things you'll need:

- a balloon

- Blow up the balloon.
- The children lie on their backs in a circle.
- The first child puts the balloon between his feet and passes it to his neighbor. Anyone who drops the balloon has to leave the circle!

Happy, Scared, Angry

4-5 years

- First practice different facial expressions with your pre-schooler. Can he look very angry or very sad? Can he recognize when you look very happy?
- Now your pre-schooler can try to draw these faces.
- If you want, you can hang these pictures up and point to them when you feel happy, scared, angry, or sad.

Things you'll need:

- paper
- markers or crayons

Did you know that...

- Young children don't understand a lot about the feelings they have.
- Yet they still have very intense feelings. They might be scared of the shadows on the walls or happy because they received lots of birthday presents.
- You can help them understand their feelings by talking with them.

4-5 years

Preschool Charades

Language game

- In this game your pre-schooler can act something out without using words.
- Can he show "driving a car" or "eating" without saying a word? The one who can guess what he is showing can be the next actor.

Confetti Art

4-5 years

- Your pre-schooler can make confetti with the hole punch and the pieces of colored paper. Collect all the confetti on the tray.
- Make a picture with the glue on the paper. Turn the paper over and press it in the layer of confetti. Turn the paper back over to see the special drawing.

Things you'll need:

- a hole punch
- pieces of colored paper
- paper
- glue
- a tray

4-5 years

Tasty Necklace

Things you'll need:

- popcorn, raisins, or candies with a hole
- thread
- a darning needle

- Thread the needle and string on the popcorn, raisins, or candy.
- Tie the ends together and you have a nice edible necklace for your pre-schooler.
- Of course, the needle is not a toy for your little one!

Silhouettes

4-5 years

- Hang the sheet in the room–for instance, in the door opening.
- Place the light behind the sheet.
- One person sits down on the side without the light. The other children one by one walk behind the sheet and make funny movements. Can the other child guess who's running behind the sheet?

Things you'll need:

- a white sheet
- a lamp

Interview

4-5 years

Things you'll need:

- a voice recorder

- It's fun to record a real conversation between you and your child. It'll be a nice memory for later for both of you.

- Test in advance that your recorder works and think about the things you want to ask him. You can ask him what he likes or with whom he likes to play. You can also look together at a picture album and start a conversation this way.

Counting

4-5 years

- Cut the cards in half with a jagged edge.
- On one half, write a number from one to five. On the other half draw images corresponding to the number–for example, one fish or five clouds, etc.
- Together with your pre-schooler you can try to match the puzzle halves together. This is a fun way to practice counting together.

Things you'll need:

- cards
- felt-tip pens or markers
- a pencil
- a pair of scissors

Did you know that...

- Pre-schoolers are introduced to numbers and letters in school as part of getting ready for kindergarten.
- Children often learn counting with songs and rhythms. Learning counting and numbers now helps prepare them for math in later grades.

4-5 years

Touch and Feel Game

Things you'll need:

- a pillowcase
- different objects like a toothbrush, a cuddly toy, or a block

- Fill the pillowcase with different objects while your pre-schooler watches you.
- He can put his hands in the bag and feel which objects are in it. As soon as he guesses what the object is, he can play with it for a while.

Sorting Out Socks

4-5 years

- Hang all the socks on the edge of the laundry basket. First your little one has to try to put the socks in pairs. You might have to help him with this job.
- Then you can show him how you fold the socks together. He can try this, too.
- What's an annoying job for you becomes an challenging game for him!

Things you'll need:

- a laundry basket
- unsorted socks

Did you know that...

- Children love to help you with the housekeeping.
- Let your pre-schooler help you fold the towels or to bring the laundry to the different rooms. For you it's an extra help and for him a fun job. In addition you give him a bit of responsibility.

4-5 years

Colors of the Rainbow

Things you'll need:

- chalk
- a rubber band or tape

- Attach two or more chalk sticks together with the rubber band or the tape.
- Now your pre-schooler can draw a nice rainbow on the sidewalk. The layers of different colors will make a nice picture.

Don't Let the Balloon Fall

4-5 years

- The children have to keep the balloons in the air as long as possible. Small taps are the best way to do this.
- As soon as the balloon touches the ground, you're out.

Things you'll need:

- balloons

4-5 years

Island Hopping

Things you'll need:

- pillows or newspapers

- Put different pillows or newspapers on the ground with distances between them.
- These pillows are islands between which you can hop.
- Of course you can not jump in the water! Watch out for sharks!

Play Dough

4-5 years

- Mix the flour with the salt in the bowl. Add the oil and the water. Mix everything. Make sure you don't have lumps.
- Now you have play dough which you can use to make shapes. By rolling little snakes you can also make letters. You can help your pre-schooler form the letters of his name.
- Bake the letters 1 or 2 hours in a low heat oven.
- When the letters have cooled down, your pre-schooler can paint them.

Things you'll need:

- a bowl
- 2 cups of flour
- 2 cups of salt
- 2 spoonfuls of vegetable oil
- 1 cup of water
- an oven
- paint
- a paintbrush

Did you know that...

- Children from this age learn and recognize the letters from their name.
- Spelling their names comes slowly. In kindergarten they will become masters at writing their names.

4-5 years

Eating Your Own Name

Things you'll need:

- any food with letters (for example, alphabet soup, pasta, or cookies)

- Serve your child the alphabet food.
- Can your pre-schooler pick out the letters of his name? Of course now he gets to eat them!